WOLFERL

the first six years in the life of
Wolfgang Amadeus Mozart
1756-1762

LISL WEIL
Holiday House / New York

For Thomas and Timmy, with love

Library of Congress Cataloging-in-Publication Data
Weil, Lisl.
Wolferl : the first six years in the life of
Wolfgang Amadeus Mozart, 1756–1762 /
written and illustrated by Lisl Weil.—1st ed.
p. cm.
Summary: A portrait of the great composer as
a child prodigy who astounded the courts
of Europe with his musical genius.
ISBN 0-8234-0876-0
1. Mozart, Wolfgang Amadeus, 1756–1791—Juvenile literature.
2. Composers—Austria—Biography—Juvenile literature.
[1. Mozart, Wolfgang Amadeus, 1756–1791—Childhood and youth.
2. Composers.]
I. Title.
ML3930.M9W28   1991
780′.92—dc20
[B]   90-47684   CIP   AC MN
ISBN 0-8234-0876-0

"God has let a miracle see the light in Salzburg. . . . And if it ever is to become my duty to convince the world of this miracle, the time is now, when people ridicule and deny all miracles."

—Leopold Mozart, letter to Lorenz Hagenauer
July 30, 1768

On a wintry evening on Sunday, January 27, 1756, a baby boy was born in Salzburg, Austria. His parents were overjoyed. They thanked God for their good fortune. The baby was their seventh child, but only the second one to live.

Wolferl grew up at a time when Austria was a grand and wealthy country, ruled by the great empress Maria Theresa in the splendid city of Vienna.

Wolferl's father, Leopold Mozart, was the head composer at the court of Prince-archbishop Sigismund of Salzburg. He was also the court's assistant *Kapellmeister* or music director. He helped to choose the music that would be played in churches and chapels and also at festivals and balls. Even though Leopold worked for the bishop, he didn't earn much money. In order to make more, he gave music lessons.

Besides teaching music to students who came to the house, Papa Mozart taught Nannerl to play the clavier and violin.

The Mozart house was always filled with music. Wolferl could hear it from his cradle. He could listen to it as he took his first steps. He could stand on his tiptoes and touch the keyboards. How he loved all the music!

When Wolferl was just three years old, he could play by ear. If he heard a piece of music, he could sit down and play what he'd heard without practicing beforehand.

Wolferl began to accompany Nannerl as she played her violin. His parents were astonished by how well he could play.

One day, Papa Mozart and his musician friends were preparing for a concert. Wolferl ran into the room, holding his violin.

"Let me play too. Please, Papa, please!"

At first his father said no, but Wolferl kept asking. Finally, Papa Mozart agreed.

To everyone's amazement, Wolferl played along perfectly on the violin.

When Wolferl was playing music, he was well behaved. But at other times, he was full of mischief. He loved to tease Nannerl. Sometimes he dressed up as a ghost and scared her.

Wolferl began to compose his own melodies when he was about four years old. They were lovely, short pieces that Papa wrote down in his notebook. It was then that Mama and Papa began to think that "God daily works wonders with our child."

Papa Mozart decided it was time to teach Wolferl to write down music, to read music, and to learn about how musical instruments worked.

Wolferl took to his lessons with the greatest of ease—just like a little bird takes to flying.

Papa thought it might be difficult for Wolferl to pump the pedals on the organ. But no—Wolferl stood on his tiptoes and pushed the pedals so well, it seemed that he had practiced for months!

The people of Salzburg began talking about the talented Mozart children. They were particularly taken by Wolferl, the small boy who composed such wonderful melodies.

Even Prince-archbishop Sigismund became curious. He invited the Mozart children to perform at his palace. The archbishop was known to be a stern man, but when he heard the children's music, he was enchanted. He thought that young Wolferl's compositions sounded like the voices of angels.

Soon many of the noble families in Salzburg were inviting Nannerl and Wolferl to perform. However, Papa let the children give concerts only occasionally, as he wanted to leave Wolferl enough time to compose and practice at home.

Mama hustled and bustled to get the children ready when they had a performance. "Take good care of your brother," she'd tell Nannerl. "Don't let him eat too many sweets and watch out that his feet don't get wet on rainy or snowy days."

The children enjoyed traveling to people's fancy houses. It was a treat to ride in the spacious travel coaches that their father rented.

Wolferl and Nannerl were glad when their music pleased the audience. And they enjoyed the delicious meals that were served afterwards. Papa was happy, too, because the noble patrons would pay to hear the children play. But Papa Mozart dreamed of still more for his children, especially Wolferl. His hopes went higher and higher.

Finally, Papa arranged for his family to go on a big trip. On September 18, 1762, they left for Vienna. The children had a wonderful time traveling by boat down the Danube River.

Wolferl and Nannerl became the sensation of Vienna. People everywhere raved about their music, particularly the compositions of "that amazing little Mozart." And then, one day, Papa Mozart's dreams came true. A special invitation arrived from the empress Maria Theresa. She invited the children to come and perform before her family at the castle Schönbrunn. She even sent over two beautiful court costumes for them to wear at the concert.

Wolferl's costume, made of the finest lavender cloth, was decorated with gold braids and buttons.

Nannerl's costume was made of white brocaded taffeta. It was decorated with lavender and pink lacy flowers.

On the morning of the performance, Mama made Nannerl practice an extra deep curtsy. She made Wolferl practice an extra deep bow. Now they were ready to be presented before the empress.

Nannerl and Wolferl played in one of the empress's private salons. Maria Theresa, her husband Francis I, and their family all listened. "The music of the children is beautiful," exclaimed the empress when they were finished.

And then something quite unexpected happened!

Very, very unexpected!

Wolferl was so happy with the way things had gone that he ran over to the empress, climbed up on her lap, and gave her a big kiss! The empress did not seem to mind. She was used to children. After all, she had given birth to sixteen of them! "Wolfgang Amadeus is such a charming and gifted child," she said. "Such great talent in such a small boy!" And Francis I called him "a little magician."

Wolferl and Nannerl were invited often to perform at Schönbrunn. After each concert, they went to a children's party at the palace. They got to eat *Kugelhupf*, an Austrian raisin cake, and chocolate *Torte* with whipped cream. Then they played hide-and-seek. One time, Wolferl tripped while trying to hide, and a little princess helped him up. Her name was Marie Antoinette, and she was seven years old. "When I grow up, perhaps I will marry her," thought Wolferl.

The Mozarts stayed on in Vienna, where Nannerl and Wolferl continued to perform.

But then cold and nasty weather set in and people began to catch cold.

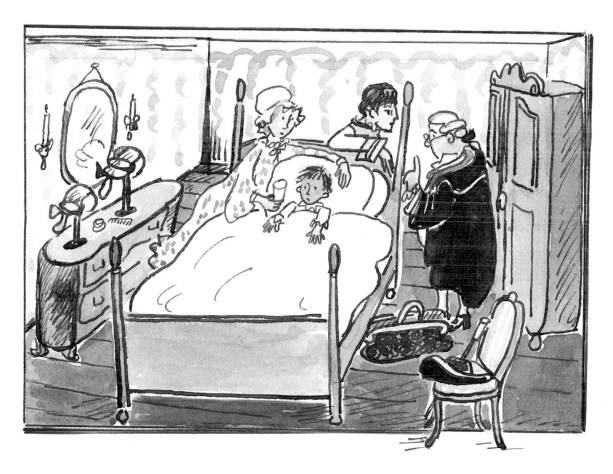

After another performance at Schönbrunn, Wolferl himself caught a bad cold. He also had a high fever and a rash. It was the 21st of October.

Maria Theresa sent little gifts, as did many of the other people before whom Wolferl had played. Except for the doctor, no one visited. People were afraid that they might catch Wolferl's sickness.

Wolferl had to stay in bed for almost a month. Finally, he became well enough to travel. The Mozarts returned home to Salzburg on January 5, 1763.

Still weak and tired, Wolferl was sorry that his wonderful time in Vienna had drawn to an end. He felt that nothing would ever happen again in his life that would be as wonderful. We, of course, know more . . .

Wolferl

Wolferl went on to become known as Wolfgang Amadeus Mozart, one of the world's greatest and most beloved composers. In his short life, he composed a wealth of concertos, sonatas, chamber music, symphonies, operas, *Singspiels*, church music, contra dances, and *Divertimentis*.

Wolfgang Amadeus Mozart
1756 — 1791

Although Mozart's talent was celebrated and recognized when he was a child, it was envied by many as he became an adult. He died when he was just thirty-five years old. Only a few family members and friends went to his funeral. No one followed his coffin to the grave, where he was buried a pauper.

But his music has lived on and is loved by people everywhere.

Wolferl

GLOSSARY

Chamber music: Music to be performed in a private room.

Clavier: A stringed keyboard instrument, such as the harpsichord.

Composition: Music that a musician writes down from his or her imagination.

Contra dance: Music for a folk dance.

Danube River: A major river in Europe that flows through West Germany, Austria, Hungary, Romania, and Russia before emptying into the Black Sea.

Divertimento: A kind of chamber music.

Francis I: The husband of Maria Theresa of Austria. He served as The Holy Roman Emperor from 1745 to 1765.

Hagenauer, Lorenz: The Mozarts' landlord in Salzburg. Leopold wrote him a series of letters during the family's trip to Vienna, September 18, 1762 to January 5, 1763.

Kapellmeister: The director of a choir or orchestra.

Kugelhupf: A sugary raisin cake that often contains nuts and fruit, too.

Maria Theresa: A member of the wealthy Hapsburg family who ruled Vienna during part of the 18th century.

Marie Antoinette: Born in Vienna November 2, 1755, she went on to marry King Louis XVI of France. She was the daughter of Maria Theresa and Francis I.

Melody: A series of tones that, when played one after another, makes a fine tune.

Patron: One who uses his or her wealth to help support the arts or another noble cause.

Schönbrunn: The Austrian palace that was built for Maria Theresa and her father Charles VI.

Sigismund, Prince-archbishop: The chief bishop in the city of Salzburg during Mozart's early life.

Singspiel: A musical play.

Torte: A flat pastry often filled with jam or chocolate cream and covered with frosting and whipped cream.

Vienna: The capital of Austria.

The Clavichord

Empress Maria Theresa